KINGFISHER READERS

level
4

Spiders

Claire Llewellyn

KINGFISHER
NEW YORK

KINGFISHER
LONDON & NEW YORK

Distributed in the U.S. and Canada by Macmillan,
175 Fifth Ave., New York, NY 10010

Library of Congress Cataloging-in-Publication data
has been applied for.

Series editor: Thea Feldman
Literacy consultant: Ellie Costa, Bank Street School for Children, New York

ISBN: 978-0-7534-7150-0 (HB)
ISBN: 978-0-7534-7151-7 (PB)

Kingfisher books are available for special promotions
and premiums. For details contact: Special Markets
Department, Macmillan, 175 Fifth Ave., New York, NY 10010.

For more information, please visit
www.kingfisherbooks.com

Printed in China
9 8 7 6 5 4 3 2 1
1TR/0314/WKT/UG/105MA

Picture credits
The Publisher would like to thank the following for permission to reproduce their material. Every care has
been taken to trace copyright holders. However, if there have been unintentional omissions or failure to trace
copyright holders, we apologize and will, if informed, endeavor to make corrections in any future edition.
Top = t; Bottom = b; Center = c; Left = l; Right = r
Cover Shutterstock (SS)/FloridaStock and pages 3t SS/Audrey Snider-Bell: 3ct SS/Fong Kam Yee:
3c SS/Cathy Keifer: 3cb SS/Kletr: 3b FLPA/Paul Hobson; 4 SS/Tolchik; 5t FLPA/Richard Becker;
5b SS/Audrey Snider-Bell; 6l SS/Henrik Larsson; 6c SS/alslutsky; 6r SS/FloridaStock; 7t Getty/
Stan Osolinksi/OSF; 7c Shutterstock/efendy; 7bl Getty/Roger de la Harpe/Gallo Images; 7br SS/D.
Kucharski & K. Kucharska; 8–9 KF Archive; 9t Nature/Jose B. Ruiz; 10 Nature/Kim Taylor; 11 FLPA/
Malcolm Schuyl; 12 KF Archive; 13 SS/neelsky; 14 FLPA/Heidi & Hans-Juergen Koch; 15t SS/Cathy
Keifer; 15c Getty/Photolibrary; 15b SS/Hulb Theunissen; 16 SS/Fong Kam Yee; 17t SS/Jason Patrick
Ross; 17b FLPA/Piotr Nasrecki/Minden; 18 FLPA/Photo Researchers; 19t Nature/Stephen Dalton;
19b FLPA/Paul Hobson; 20 SS/Nate A.; 21t Nature/Photo Researchers; 21c Photoshot/NHPA;
21b SS/Miles Boyer; 22 Getty/Jerry Young/DK; 23 Alamy/Zach Holmes; 24 SS/Kletr;
25t SS/Kurt_G; 25b Nature/Stephen Dalton; 26t FLPA/Chien Lee/Minden; 26b Shutterstock/Andrey
Pavlov; 27t Nature/Premaphotos; 27b FLPA/Richard Becker; 28l Alamy/Kristen Soper; SS/Giuliano
C. Del Moretto; 29 Corbis/Matthias Schrader/dpa; 31 SS/Fong Kam Yee.

Contents

All about spiders

There are billions of spiders on Earth. They live in houses and gardens, ponds and caves, rainforests, deserts, and the Arctic. They survive in almost every possible **habitat**, except for **Antarctica** and the oceans.

So far, scientists have found about 38,000 different **species** of spiders. New species are being discovered all the time, so there may be many more than this. Every spider catches animals for food. The largest eat snakes, lizards, and birds. The smallest eat tiny flies.

Many spiders live among plants in parks and gardens.

Raft spiders live near marshes and ponds.
They catch insects on the water's surface.

This book is all about spiders. It tells you how they spin silk, how they produce their young, and all the different ways they catch and kill their **prey**.

Leg span

0 inches
(0 cm)

10 inches
(25 cm)

Biggest and smallest

The world's largest spider is the Goliath tarantula, shown here. It has a **leg span** of nearly 10 inches (25 cm). The smallest is the Samoan moss spider. With a leg span of less than 0.02 inches (0.5 mm), it can hardly be seen.

Spiders and their relatives

Spiders belong to a large group of animals called **arachnids**. All arachnids have four pairs of legs and a body that is divided into two parts. Other arachnids include harvestmen, scorpions, mites, and ticks. They are close relatives of spiders.

Spider   Insect

Not an insect!

What's the difference between a spider and an insect? Spiders have two parts to their body and eight legs. Insects have three parts to their body and six legs. Most insects have **antennas** and wings; spiders never do.

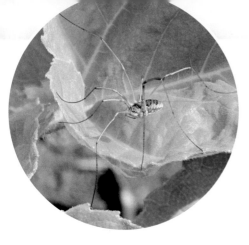

A harvestman has long, thin legs, but it lacks the waist that a spider has.

A scorpion has a long, **segmented** body, a large pair of claws, and a curved tail with a stinger at the tip.

A mite is tiny, with short legs and a round body. Many mites can live on animals and irritate their skin.

A tick clings on to animals and feeds on their blood. Ticks can spread disease.

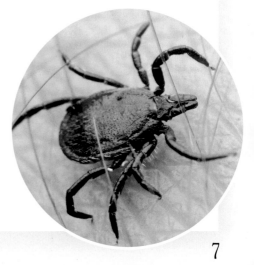

A spider's body

A spider's body is made up of two main segments: the head and the **abdomen**. The two parts are joined by a slender waist.

Head

Fangs are sharp.

Palps are for tasting and feeling.

Hairs feel tiny movements of other animals.

The whole body is covered with a tough, outer coat called the exoskeleton. This does not grow with the spider. Instead, as the spider gets bigger, the exoskeleton bursts.

Eyes: spiders have two, four, six, or eight eyes.

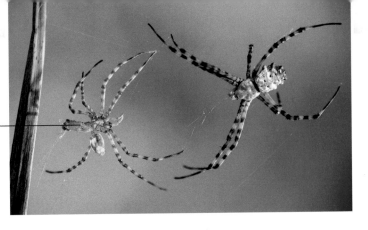

Old coat

Underneath there is a new, larger coat. The spider crawls out of the old coat and leaves it behind. This is called molting.

Legs are long and segmented.

Abdomen

Feet at the end of each leg allow spiders to grip on to things.

Spinnerets produce silk.

Speedy spiders

Spiders are very quick, thanks to their eight long legs. The giant house spider holds the record for the fastest spider. It can move nearly 21 inches (53 cm) per second!

Spider silk

Spider silk is an amazing material. It is finer than hair, stronger than steel, and stretchy like elastic. It is waterproof and light enough to float.

Spiders use silk in all sorts of ways: to build their webs, line their **burrows**, protect their eggs, and wrap up their prey. They also make silk safety lines to escape from danger or jump distances.

A jumping spider leaps into the air from its silk safety line.

Thick and thin

A spider's silk is not always the same. It can be thick or thin, wet or dry, sticky or wool-like. It all depends on how it will be used.

A garden spider pulls the silk from its spinnerets to wrap up a fly it has caught in its web.

A spider makes silk inside its body in special **organs** called glands. The runny silk squirts out of holes in the spinnerets, like water out of a showerhead. The spider then uses one of its legs to pull and twist the different strands into a single, solid thread.

Spider webs

Many spiders make sticky webs to catch flies and other insects. Spiders spin webs in a variety of shapes, such as flat sheets, long tubes, and round **orb webs**.

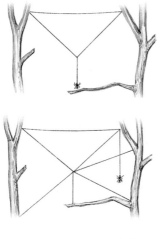

Making an orb web

1. The spider connects two twigs with strong thread and pulls the thread down.

2. It adds spokes and fixes them firmly.

3. Then it spins a sticky spiral to hold the spokes in place.

An orb web takes about an hour to make. The lacy threads are soon spoiled by dust, wind, or rain, so most spiders spin a new web every day. The old one does not go to waste; the spider eats it and **recycles** the silk.

Record breaker

The golden orb-weaver spider spins the largest orb web in the world. It builds webs more than 3 feet (1 m) wide that are strong enough to catch all kinds of insects and even some frogs and birds!

A helpless fly is rolled up in silk by a garden spider.

Deadly fangs

When an insect flies into a web, the spider feels it right away through the fine hairs on its legs. It darts out quickly to bite its prey.

Nearly all spiders produce **venom**. As they bite their prey, venom pumps out through their hollow fangs and enters their prey's body. The venom does two things: it stops the creature from moving and begins to break down its body, turning it into a soupy liquid. The spider then sucks it up.

If a large insect flies into the web, the spider quickly wraps it in silk before biting it. This prevents the insect from breaking free. If the spider isn't hungry, it will keep its prisoner waiting and return to eat it later.

A black and yellow garden spider wraps up a grasshopper before it can get away.

Types of fangs

Some spiders have fangs that point toward each other, like pincers. They are good for seizing prey. Other spiders have fangs that point downward, like daggers. These spiders have to lift their head up and strike down to attack.

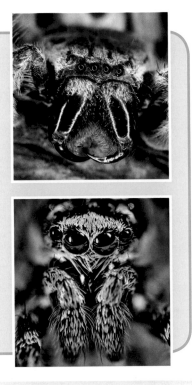

Hunting spiders

Not all spiders spin webs. Some hunt for a meal. Hunting spiders are strong and fast and have sharp eyesight to spot their prey.

Jumping spiders are deadly hunters. They have excellent eyesight and can jump up to 50 times their body length to catch their prey.

A jumping spider prepares to pounce on its insect prey.

Amazing eyes

Jumping spiders have two big eyes on the front of their head and smaller eyes around the sides. The large eyes see things very clearly. The smaller eyes spot prey and judge how far away it is.

A fishing spider feels for prey in the water.

The fishing spider hunts at the river's edge. Its front legs rest on the surface of the water, feeling for the movement of tadpoles, frogs, and fish in the water.

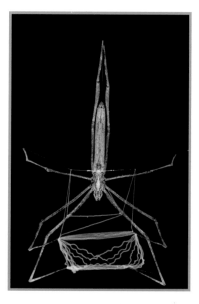

A net-casting spider prepares to catch its prey.

Net-casting spiders hunt at night. They hold a small flat web between their legs and throw it over insects like a net as they pass by.

Ambush!

Some spiders **ambush** their prey. They hide somewhere safe and keep very still. Then, when they see their prey, they jump out and grab it!

The trapdoor spider digs a burrow with a trapdoor on the top. At night, it opens the door a crack and waits for an insect to pass by. Then it jumps on the insect and drags it back into its burrow.

A trapdoor spider leaps out of its burrow to grab an unlucky insect.

If you look closely, you can see the fang of a purse-web spider that has just stabbed this cranefly from beneath.

The purse-web spider makes a long silk tube and covers it with bits of soil. The spider hides inside the tube and waits for its prey to walk over it. Then it stabs its prey through the soft, silk walls before dragging it inside.

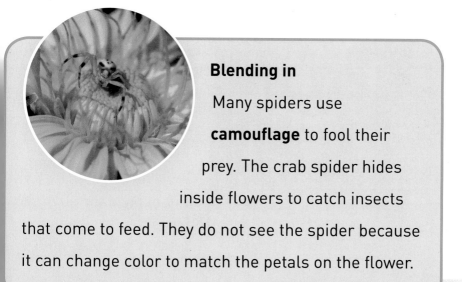

Blending in

Many spiders use **camouflage** to fool their prey. The crab spider hides inside flowers to catch insects that come to feed. They do not see the spider because it can change color to match the petals on the flower.

19

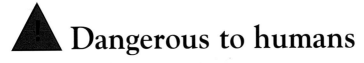 Dangerous to humans

Nearly every species of spider has its own kind of venom, but only about 100 species are dangerous to humans. Venom affects humans in different ways. Some venom affects the muscles and causes painful cramps. Other venom causes damage around the bite itself, leaving scars that take months to heal. Luckily, most bites can be treated with special medicines.

Black widow spider

Watch out for: red markings on abdomen

Found in: warm parts of the world, including the southern U.S.

Leg span: 1.5 inches (3.8 cm)

Effect of venom: breathing problems, muscle cramps, and vomiting

Brazilian wandering spider

Watch out for: large, brown, hairy body

Found in: tropical rainforests of South America

Leg span: 4.7 inches (12 cm)

Effect of venom: severe pain. Can be fatal.

Sydney funnel-web spider

Watch out for: shiny, brown-black body

Found in: eastern Australia

Leg span: 2.4 inches (6 cm)

Effect of venom: sickness and vomiting. Can kill in under two hours.

Brown recluse spider

Watch out for: violin-like markings on its head

Found in: southern U.S. and Mexico

Leg span: 0.4–0.8 inches (1–2 cm)

Effect of venom: a deep wound that is slow to heal

Finding a mate

Most spiders live alone. When it is time to mate, a male finds a female by following a scent she leaves on her silk.

The male spider is often much smaller than the female. If he is not careful, she could mistake him for prey and eat him. So, as he approaches the female, he may give her an insect to eat or tap a friendly signal on her web. If she accepts him, the two spiders mate.

Eggs for life

After mating just once, the female black widow spider can lay eggs for the rest of her life.

A week or two later, the female lays her eggs. She wraps them in a thick **cocoon** and then puts them somewhere safe to hatch. Most females leave before their young hatch.

Little and large: a male
golden orb-weaver spider
carefully approaches
a female that is much
larger than himself.

Baby wasp spiders hatch together.

Baby spiders

Baby spiders are called **spiderlings**. They hatch out of their eggs together but soon spread out to look for food. If they didn't, they would eat each other! Each tiny spiderling makes a line of very fine silk, called gossamer, and uses it to float away on the breeze. This is called ballooning.

Most spider mothers do not care for their young, but the wolf spider mother is different. She carries her egg cocoon around with her. After hatching, the spiderlings climb on her back.

Wolf spiderlings cling to their mother as she runs and hunts.

They ride there for a week or so until they are big enough to hunt. If one of them falls off, the mother stops whatever she is doing and helps it climb back on.

Ballooning

Ballooning helps spiders get to new places. A spider cannot control where or how far it will go. That is up to the wind. Some spiders wind up traveling for hundreds of miles!

Spider defenses

Spiders are food for birds, lizards, centipedes, wasps, and many other animals. Most spiders escape from their enemies by dropping away on a line of silk. Others have special **defenses**.

Some spiders copy ants by walking on six legs and holding up the other two so that they look like antennas. Birds don't like the taste of ants, so they leave these spiders alone.

A jumping spider copies an ant.

A tarantula defends itself by flicking hairs on the face of an enemy. The hairs have sharp little hooks, which stick into the enemy's eyes and nose and make them feel itchy and sore.

Ant

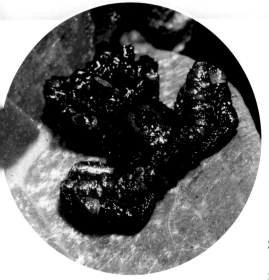

The bird-dropping spider looks like . . . a bird dropping! This is great camouflage, and most hungry animals pass right by it.

A bird-dropping spider looks nothing like a spider!

Deadly enemy

Spiders' defenses don't always work. The spider-hunting wasp is a spider's deadly enemy. It stings a spider so that it cannot move and then lays its eggs inside the spider's body. Hungry **grubs** hatch out of the eggs and eat the spider alive.

A spider-hunting wasp (on the left) drags a wolf spider back to its burrow.

Spiders help us

Many people do not like spiders, but they help us in many ways. They eat billions of the mosquitoes, cockroaches, and other insects that cause disease. They also eat many pests in gardens and on farms. Without spiders, swarms of insects would feed on our crops and people would starve.

Grasshoppers are a pest on farms because they eat crops. Spiders are a natural form of pest control.

Tasty tarantulas

In some parts of South America and Southeast Asia, people eat roasted tarantulas. They have a nutty flavor.

Scientists in Germany work to copy spider silk and produce it in the laboratory.

Spiders may be very useful in the future. Scientists are studying spider venom in the hope of using it in **insecticides** and to replace harmful chemicals. They are also studying how spiders make silk. This amazing material may have many uses. We may be able to use it for car seat belts, parachutes, and bulletproof clothing. One day, doctors may even sew up wounds using spider silk!

Healing webs

Stories from thousands of years ago tell how people once used spider webs to help heal their wounds.

Glossary

abdomen the back part of an arachnid's body

ambush to lie in wait and attack by surprise

Antarctica the ice-covered land around the South Pole

antennas the pair of feelers on an insect's head

arachnids a group of animals that have four pairs of legs and a body divided into two parts

burrows holes or tunnels dug by an animal

camouflage the color or markings of an animal that help it blend in with its surroundings

cocoon the silky covering a spider spins to protect its eggs. Other animals make different types of cocoons.

defenses the ways that animals protect themselves from attack

grubs the tiny creatures that hatch out of insects' eggs. Also called larvae

habitat the home of an animal in nature

insecticides the sprays and powders that farmers use to kill insect pests

leg span the distance between the tips of two legs on the opposite sides of a spider

orb webs webs with a round, circular shape

organs the parts of an animal's body, such as the eyes or glands, that do a particular job

prey animals that are hunted and killed by other animals for food

recycles uses again or makes new from used materials

segmented made up of different parts or segments

species a group of living things that share similar features and can mate and have babies

spiderlings baby spiders

spinnerets the parts of a spider's body that produce silk

venom the poison that a spider or other animal injects when it bites

Index